P9-CQF-801

11/08

DATE DUE

BECOMING
BILLIE
HOLIDAY

Carole Boston Weatherford

ART BY

Floyd Cooper

WORDSONG

Honesdale, Pennsylvania

For Ron, Mommy, Caresse, and Jeffrey
—C.B.W.

Text copyright © 2008 by Carole Boston Weatherford
Illustrations copyright © 2008 by Floyd Cooper
All rights reserved
Printed in China
Designed by Helen Robinson
First edition

CIP data is available

WORDSONG
An Imprint of Boyds Mills Press, Inc.
815 Church Street
Honesdale, Pennsylvania 18431

When you listen to her, it's almost like an audiotape of her autobiography. She didn't sing anything unless she had lived it.
—Tony Bennett, jazz singer

CONTENTS

Note: Unless marked with an asterisk (*), poems borrow
titles from Billie Holiday's songs.

Intro: What Shall I Say?

The way Mom toted around
that magazine with my photo inside,
you'd have thought
I was Woman of the Year.
I don't blame Sadie. Wasn't every day
that a colored face, let alone
her only child, appeared in *Time*.
I was proud too till I read
what that two-bit critic wrote.
Called me "roly-poly"; said I wouldn't diet,
was stuck on my own voice,
and cared for tunes but not the words.
What did he know
about my taste in food or music?
I never even talked to the cat,
but he'd better not cross my path.
If he dares, he'll get a mouthful,
hear just how I got to Harlem
and became Lady Day.
Oh, the tales I'd tell.

Why Was I Born?

Because Sadie had one day off a week
from her job as a live-in maid
and crammed as many thrills as she could
into the few hours she called her own.

'Cause teenagers flocked to the carnival in July
for rides, cotton candy, and sideshows.

'Cause Clarence had rested his banjo
for the evening, hoping to sneak a peek
under the tent during the burlesque show.

'Cause he and Sadie bumped into each other
at the hot-dog stand and shimmied
all night long in the sultry summer air.

'Cause Clarence whispered in Sadie's ear,
sweet-talked his way right up her skirt.

'Cause that one time was all it took
for two dumb kids to make a baby.

'Cause Sadie went to Philly with full belly
to keep from shaming her Baltimore kin.

'Cause I could not wait a minute longer
to burst on the scene, and 2:30 a.m.,
April 7, 1915, was as good a time as any
to gasp my first breath, cry my first chord.

'Cause I no more chose my folks
than chose my name—
Eleanora.

Love Me or Leave Me

I was two weeks old
when Mom sent
for her daddy's folks;
the same ones who
shut the door
on her as a child
when *her* daddy got a girl
from the wrong side
of the tracks in trouble.

Mom knew they wanted
no part of her,
but she hoped they'd take me
off her hands. She couldn't be
a live-in maid and nurse a child.
She turned to her half-sister Eva,
betting that blood
was thicker than shame.
But Eva had just wed
and didn't want a crying baby
spoiling her honeymoon.

So Aunt Eva's new husband
rode up to Philly
and carried me to Baltimore.
Baby in tow, he showed up,
like a stray dog,
on his mama's doorstep.
Miss Martha took me in
and cared for me,
just as she had
other neighborhood kids
down on their luck
and without a home.
I came to call her
Grandma Martha.

My First Impression of You

Tall, dark, and dashing
distant relative passing through
with empty pockets and promises.

You pinched my cheeks
and bounced me on your knee,
but music was your sweetie pie.

You were the envelopes Mom kissed,
the letters she read over and over,
and the dollar bill she tucked in her bra.

You were the one she blamed when rent
was due and I needed new shoes;
the thief who stole her heart and her youth.

A happy-go-lucky, banjo-playin',
whiskey-swiggin' papa—
gone in the blink of an eye.

How Could You?

How could you
pack your banjo
and big-band wishes
and run to New York,
leaving Mom to care
for me as best
she could alone
without a cent from you?
What kind of father
would do that,
Clarence Holiday?
Not that you ever
came around much
even before you left.

One, Two, Button Your Shoe

When I was five
I wore high-top shoes
rather than heels,
cotton frocks
rather than furs,
and white bows
instead of gardenias.

Missa Cantata / Sung Mass

In Sadie's house,
there was none of that
Bible-thumping, hand-clapping,
holy-rolling kind of religion.

We were staunch Catholics
who lit candles before saints, ate fish
on Fridays, and had the priest
over for Sunday lunch.

At St. Francis Xavier,
the oldest black Catholic church
in all of the United States,
I was baptized with holy water.

Between Latin chants, I kneeled
while Mom prayed Hail Marys.
I knew how to cross myself
before I could tie my shoes.

Left Alone

Soon as I got used
to having Mom around,
she was gone again.
She left town
more times
than I can count,
each time leaving me
in different hands.
Grandma Martha,
Aunt Eva,
Miss Vi,
and Miss Lu
did their best by me,
but they had troubles, too.
Mostly,
I was on my own.

Say It Isn't So

Love, oh love, oh careless love,
Love, oh love, oh careless love,
Love, oh love, oh careless love,
Can't you see what love has done to me?

I love my mama an' my papa, too.
I love my mama an' my papa, too.
I love my mama an' my papa, too.
Gonna leave 'em both an' go wid you.

What, oh what will mama say,
What, oh what will mama say,
What, oh what will mama say
When she learns I've gone astray?

Aunt Eva frowned on the bawdy songs
I learned from kids at school.
In her house, only hymns allowed.
She'd wash inside my mouth with soap
whenever I broke that rule.
I can still taste those nasty bubbles.

Eeny Meeny Miney Mo

I didn't have china dolls
in frilly dresses like other girls.
All I had was a bunch of boys
with naps in their hair,
rocks in their pockets,
and holes in their knickers,
willing to let a tomboy
like me join their games.
I could beat every one
of them at stickball
and out-skate any kid
on eight wheels.
I played softball better
than any boy on the block.
I may have had pigtails,
but I struck out every Tom, Dick,
and Harry who swung a bat.
I earned my braggin' rights.

(You Ain't Gonna Bother Me) No More

I could keep up with the boys
shooting marbles and dice,
but not catching bugs.
Crawly things gave me the creeps,
and all the boys knew it.
Once, after a ballgame,
I was sitting on the curb
and a sore loser swung a rat
by the tail right in my face.
I begged him to stop,
but he just grinned.
Then that rat brushed my cheek.
I grabbed a baseball bat
and sent that boy to the hospital.

Practice Makes Perfect

At #104, Elliott Elementary,
our day began with prayer
and the Negro National Anthem,
Lift Ev'ry Voice and Sing,
and continued with the three Rs:
reading, 'riting, and 'rithmetic.

I was a caged bird at the desk,
practicing handwriting
and the times tables
and reading textbooks
cast off by white schools;
torn pages leaving gaps in stories.

While I recited a poem by heart,
the teacher paced the floor,
rapping a ruler on her palm.
In that classroom, her word was law.
She didn't think twice about using
a paddle if someone got out of line.

In gym, I learned to box,
and during recess, I scuffled
with anyone who dared
talk about my mama
or even look at me sideways.
I made the biggest bullies cry.

I can't count how many days
the teacher kept me
after school to write one hundred times:
I must not fight boys.
I must not fight boys.
I must not fight boys.

Ghost of Yesterday

My great-grandmother was older than dirt
and could spin a tale from a fleck of dust.
As a slave on a Virginia plantation,
she lived out back behind the big house
and had sixteen children by her master,
Charles Fagan. Only one lived to be grown—
my grandpop, Charlie Fagan.
Great-grandma couldn't read or write a lick,
but she recalled slavery days
and told Bible stories that she knew by heart.
She suffered from dropsy, kept
her swollen legs bound in cloths,
and had to sleep sitting up.
Some days, I bathed her after school.

One night I dreamed she begged me
to let her lie down and rest.
I laid her on a blanket on the floor
and she asked me to lie with her
to hear a story. In my dream,
I fell asleep before she finished
and I awoke in her death hold.
Neighbors broke her arm to free me.
I woke from that dream in a cold sweat.
The dead have spooked me ever since.

Don't Worry 'Bout Me

An old lady who was always
peeping out second-story windows,
nosing in everyone's business,
shook her finger at me and said,
I know what you're doing with those boys.
I wasn't studying doing the nasty.

Besides, Mom had warned me,
Neither one of us got a daddy
who gives us the time of day.
Don't make the same mistake.
I can hardly keep food on the table
and a roof over our heads.
A baby is the last thing we need.

Sailboat in the Moonlight

I dreamed Mom and Dad
married on a silver lake,
and in a cottage
on the shore, we danced as Dad
plucked his banjo and sang blues.

Havin' Myself a Time

Truth be told,
no one raised me.
I just ran wild.
The folks Mom had
looking after me
while she was gone
would get me off to school
like clockwork,
but they never knew if I went.
Most days, I didn't.
Running the streets
was more my speed.
When it came to playing
hooky, I was a quick study.

Guilty

I guess I pushed my luck.
It was only a matter of time
before a truant officer caught me
on the streets during school,
and Mom and I wound up in court.
The judge ruled that I lacked
adult supervision.

I thought, at nine, I'd outgrown
that, but in the eyes
of the law, I was a minor
and Mom, an unfit mother.
My sentence, one year
at the House of the Good Shepherd
for Colored Girls.

Entrusted to nuns—
I hoped time would fly.

Gloomy Sunday

The House of the Good Shepherd
was a drafty six-story warehouse
that scraped by on $3,000 a year.
With wayward girls under their wings,
the Sisters of the Good Shepherd were as mean
as they were penniless. If we girls disobeyed,

Mother Superior made us stand on one foot
in a corner, slammed our hands with a ruler,
or made us wear a raggedy red dress
instead of a blue- or black-caped uniform.
Between chores and chapel prayers,
we did schoolwork and needlecrafts.

I stayed to myself in the yard
and ate alone in the kitchen, careful
not to bother anyone. I rarely spoke
and tried my darndest to steer clear
of those street-wise petty criminals
who'd been raised in reform school.

After five or ten years, those girls'
hearts turned cold. Older girls
bribed younger ones with sweets
and bullied their way into their beds.
A dozen nuns turned a blind eye.
This was no place for angels.

One girl died of tuberculosis
and the nuns laid her body
in the chapel and locked me
inside as punishment
for God knows what.
That scared the devil out of me.

It's a Sin to Tell a Lie

The Sisters of the Good Shepherd
took in laundry and raised
chickens to make ends meet.
We girls all had chores:
washing and ironing linens,
making beds, mopping floors,
feeding chickens, gathering eggs,
peeling potatoes, and scouring pots.

An idle mind is the devil's workshop,
the nuns said, *and confession
is good for the soul.*

Once, in the five-and-dime store,
a pair of silk stockings called my name:
Eleanora, wanna dance?
When the clerk wasn't looking,
I balled up those stockings,
stuffed them in my pocket, and waltzed
outdoors with my heart pounding.
That wasn't the only time I stole.

God Bless the Child

The nuns called me "Madge"
to protect my identity,
but the priest called me
"my child." I was by no means
a saint but had sense enough
to know I needed saving.
So I asked to be baptized.
The priest had no idea
I was christened as a baby,
just that I was willing
to change my sinful ways.
That was good reason
to renew my ties to God.
At the altar in a white dress
and veil, I beamed like a bride.
After the priest doused
holy water on my head,
I took my First Communion,
bread and wine,
the body and blood of Christ.
Then the nuns gave me
a string of rosary beads
and a prayer book.
I slept with that book.

Back in Your Own Backyard

My silence paid off.
The nuns assumed
I'd repented

and released me
three months early
for good behavior.

Back with Mom,
back in fifth grade,
back on the streets.

A month later,
I dropped out of school
for good.

Jeepers Creepers

To earn some change
for candy or a picture show,
boys shined shoes, collected
junk, or sold *Afro* newspapers;
girls minded babies or cleaned—
in my case, front steps.
Baltimore had miles
of rowhouses and marble stoops.
And even lousy housekeepers
whose homes were filthy inside
wanted sparkling clean stoops.
That's where I walked in.
The going rate for scrubbing steps
was five cents. I figured I could
double my money if I brought
my own bucket and brush.
I went from door to door,
block to block with my offer.
When someone balked at fifteen cents,
I'd throw in a bathroom
or kitchen floor for free.
Some days, I made two bucks,
a lot of money back then.

I'll Never Be the Same

On Christmas Eve, 1926,
Mom and her boyfriend Wee Wee
had gone out on the town,
leaving me home alone.
Our neighbor Mr. Rich
knocked on the door
and said Mom asked him
to check on me,
make sure I was okay.
But he checked
where he had no business,
put his hands where no man's
had been, and forced
his way between my legs.
That's where he was
when Mom caught him
with his pants down.
She called the police
and had him arrested.

At the police station
two doctors examined me, poked
and probed as I softly sobbed.
Mr. Rich was charged with rape.
That put Mom on trial, too.
The court sent me back
to House of the Good Shepherd,
this time as a state witness.
But the nuns made me repent
and I was baptized again—
as if the rape had torn me from God.

At the trial, the judge
sentenced Mr. Rich
to three months in jail.
Hell, I was the victim
and was locked away
almost as long.
In February, Mom borrowed money
from her father for a lawyer.
He got me released.
I walked and talked
the same as before,
but my childhood was spent.

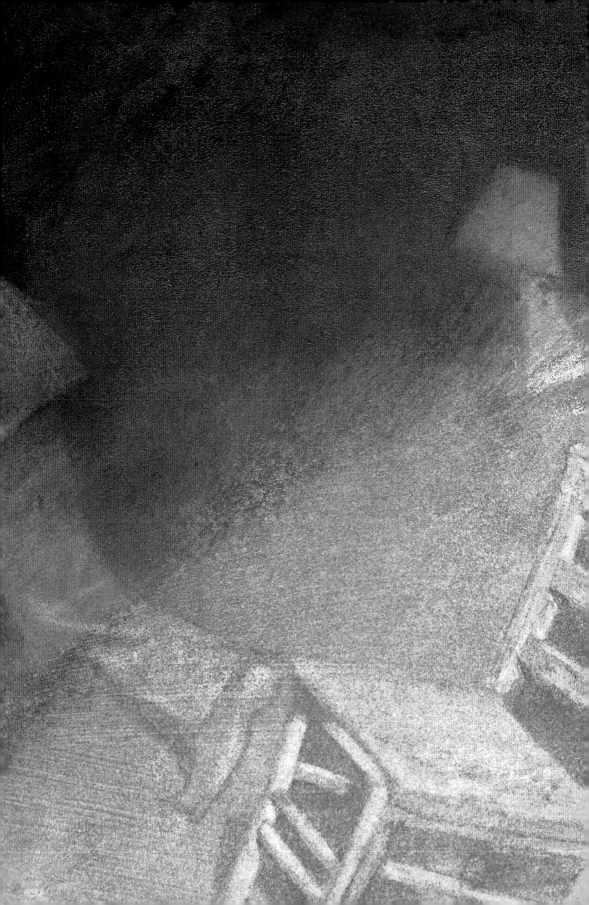

Darn That Dream

My dream was for a family;
Mom's was for a restaurant.
When she'd saved enough money
working as a maid in Roland Park
to rent a house with gas and electricity,
she hung her shingle.
The East Side Grill served
the night crowd, folks
who had not had their fill
when the clubs closed.
The house specialties: spareribs,
pigs' feet, and red beans and rice
with bootleg whiskey on the side.
I kept long hours, cooking,
waiting tables, and washing dishes.
There wasn't time
for school even if I'd cared.
I was the only help Mom had.

People of the night taught me
everything I knew.
I studied Alice Dean hard—
from her diamond rings,
Chinese furs, and satin dresses
to her wide-brimmed hats topped
with bird of paradise feathers.
The hustlers with her had
bright silk hankies blooming
in coat pockets and red garters
around their sleeves.
They flashed dollar bills,
but Alice didn't bat an eye.
She had her own money.
My dream was for a family;
Mom's was for a restaurant.
One out of two ain't bad.

I Hear Music: The Blues Are Brewin'

I was no stranger to hard work,
and Miss Alice had plenty of it
in her good-time house.
I kept busy with errands and chores—

washing basins and toilets,
changing towels, putting out
Lifebuoy soap, and peeking through
a keyhole now and then.

I got paid in tips
but would have worked for free
to wind up her Victrola
and hear music fill the room.

As Bessie Smith belted out
bar after bar, bending notes
to moods, I mouthed the words
till I knew her blues by heart.

The jazz bug bit me good
when Louis Armstrong and his Hot Five
swaggered through "West End Blues"
and turned music on its ear.

I had never heard
singing without a single word.
Scat! Dig that!
Those blues sure were brewin'.

"St. Louis Blues"
by W. C. Handy, 1914

I hate to see that evening sun go down
I hate to see that evening sun go down
'Cause, my baby, he's done left this town

Feelin' tomorrow like I feel today
If I'm feelin' tomorrow like I feel today
I'll pack my truck and make my get-a-way

St. Louis woman with her diamond ring
Pulls that man around by her apron strings
If it wasn't for her and her store-bought hair
That man I love would have gone nowhere, nowhere

I got the St. Louis Blues
Blue as I can be
That man's got a heart like a rock cast in the sea
Or else he wouldn't have gone so far from me

I love my baby like a schoolboy loves his pie
Like a Kentucky colonel loves his mint 'n' rye
I love my man till the day I die

It's the Same Old Story

I knew from Mom's tone of voice:

I gotta earn a living.
It's hard with no man around.
You obey your Aunt Eva.
Don't be a bother to Miss so-and-so.
I wish things were different.
We're gonna have a fine place one day.
I promise.

I had heard that song before;
Mom was leaving me again.

But Beautiful

Mom worked as a live-in maid,
cleaning rich people's homes,
but you'd never know by my closet.
I was sharp as a tack,
even when we barely had
two nickels to rub together.
Mom sewed some of my dresses
and sent me hand-me-downs
from rich white folks up North:
gingham skirts, pleated dresses,
and puffy-sleeved satin blouses.
All dressed up, I was the cat's meow.

Ave Maria

Organ quiet, the priest chanted
Latin prayers of consecration,
consolation, or reconciliation—
mysteries I knew nothing of.
The church replied in song.

I prayed for my mother
to stay put for a while,
my father to stick around
for more than a few hours,
and a place to call home.

I Wished on the Moon

I may have been poor,
may have been orphaned
half the time,
but for five cents
I could lose myself
in a bargain matinee.

Sitting front-row center
at the colored theater,
I imagined myself
a damsel in satin,
dripping in diamonds,
safe in the hero's arms.

Those movies
may have been black-and-white,
but my dream was Technicolor.
I left the dark theater,
squinting in broad daylight,
stars in my eyes.

If My Heart Could Only Talk

On the corner,
rent-party music
poured from windows,
churchgoers strutted by
in Sunday-best dress,
and street vendors
hawked hard crabs
and roasted peanuts
as trolleys clattered past.
On the corner of innocence
and knowledge, I posed,
hand on my hip,
whispering to a friend
about boys I liked
but lacked the nerve to tell.

Ain't Nobody's Business If I Do

At eleven, I had the body
of a grown woman,
the mouth of a sailor, and a temper
hot enough to fry an egg.

What I didn't have
was anyone to hug me,
to tuck me in at night,
or kiss me hello and good-bye.

So I got noticed the only way
I knew—cursing and screaming
in the streets, picking fights
with anyone half as mad as me.

For me, the back
of a hand was better
than the back of a head,
better than being ignored.

No Good Man: I'm a Fool to Want You

I was tall and plump with big breasts.
Men twice my age turned their heads
and wagged their tongues as I walked past.
Nice fellas who earned an honest buck
working in packing houses
wished I would look their way,
but I had no use for country boys.
I fancied hotheaded hustlers
in pinstripe suits and wingtip shoes—
men I had no business fooling with:
Burley, the amateur boxer;
Penny, the piano player;
Charlie, who ran a poolroom;
Willie, who blew every dollar
he ever made; Tidy and Beans,
both pimps; and Douglas,
a moocher without an ounce of shame.
Every last man had two gals on the side.

I'm Painting the Town Red

I was a moth, and the fast life, a flame.
Evenings found me at house parties,
small clubs, and speakeasies, sipping
white lightning and smoking weed
with night owls who didn't suspect my age.
One night, I sang a blues I'd learned
while listening to Victrolas.
My chirping hushed the chatter,
and the night crowd clapped for more.
With a half-dozen songs,
I made the rounds at Club Paradise,
Buddy Love's, Miss Ella's,
and Pop Major's and was a regular
at Ethel Moore's good-time house.
She was like a big sister to me,
and piano players, like brothers.
In shady after-hours spots,
I found a voice to grow into
and someplace to belong.

Trav'lin' Light

I toted my songs
like a satchel and felt most
at home when I sang.

You Go to My Head

I sang my songs so much
that they became
the soundtrack for my dreams,
the melody of my moods,
a room I lived in,
and a balm for my wounds.

I sang my songs enough
to know them backward
and forward, enough
to wonder if they could lift me
from hometown haunts
to center stage.

I'd sung my songs enough
to think I could take on
Baltimore's best talent
at the Harlem Theatre
Amateur Hour
and maybe even win.

If you sing a song enough,
it can go to your head that way.

Trav'lin' All Alone

Staying out till all hours at clubs
and coming in bruised or tipsy,
I wore out my welcome at Miss Lu's.
She wrote Mom a letter
telling her to come get me.
Mom sent for me instead.
I fastened a white dress with a red belt,
and Wee Wee took me to Penn Station.
With a basket of fried chicken
and a suitcase full of hard luck,
I boarded the passenger car
for my first train ride and first trip
out of town. I may as well have been
Lindbergh crossing the Atlantic.
And I was only twelve.

Bridge: I Cover the Waterfront

As I gazed out the train window
I remembered where I'd lived.

I started out on North Barnes Street
with my grandmother, Martha,
who was really no kin but was
Mom's half-sister's mother-in-law.
Then Mom and I moved in
with Aunt Eva and Uncle Robert
on Colvin Street. Aunt Eva
looked after me while Mom worked
in a factory sewing army uniforms
for soldiers off to war. Aunt Eva
was so mean I wished for marching orders.

For years, I bounced from house to house.
When Mom married Philip Gough,
my first stepdaddy, and set up house
on East Street, I stayed with Aunt Eva.
After Mom's marriage broke up,
I went back with my grandmother.
Then Mom rented a room
from Viola Green at 609 Bond Street.
Miss Vi had a Victrola, a player piano,
and a son, Freddie—a brother to me.
Weekends, we ate eggs, bacon, tripe
fried in batter, and hot biscuits
with a bowl of molasses on the side.
Mom went away on weekends
and missed those meals.

After years of scrimping and promising,
Mom got us our own place
at Dallas and Caroline streets
near the docks in the red-light district—
a rented rowhouse with five rooms,
three downstairs and two up,
and a bathtub in the kitchen.
Our house was neat as a pin,
but the streets were rough;
fights broke out day and night.
While I was in the House of the Good Shepherd
for playing hooky, Mom moved
to the West Side, rented a place
at 1421 North Fremont Avenue.
Then we moved two blocks
to 1425 North Argyle Street, a stone's throw
from Pennsylvania Avenue,
black Baltimore's main drag.

When I was ten, Mom and I moved in
with Lucy Hill and her son
Wee Wee, my second stepdaddy.
He was a gambler and womanizer,
but Mom was sweet on him
and they rented the house next door.
I stayed on with Miss Lu,
who was too frail to climb her own stairs,
much less keep up with me.
The bath was out back and water
had to be brought indoors
from the summer kitchen,
a chore that fell on me.
The walls were so thin, I could hear
Mom and Wee Wee arguing.
Once when he stayed out all night,
Mom pulled a gun on him.

If a woman's good enough
for you to live with, she yelled,
she's good enough for you to marry.
Next thing I knew, they'd both gone
to New York, leaving me a statue
of Mary, a wall hanging of Jesus,
and a bedroom set bought on credit.
Before long, Wee Wee ran back
to Baltimore, but Mom stayed up north
in Long Branch, New Jersey, as a maid.

Every time we moved to a new place,
I'd fill a jar with holy water from church
to sprinkle the corners of the room.
Even that didn't bring good luck.
I grew up in a port city,
but never dropped anchor long.

The conductor shouted, "Philly!"
My daydream screeched to a halt.
Home was behind me now.

Autumn in New York

Mom had paid my fare
to Long Branch, New Jersey,
but my heart was set on Harlem
and my mind was made up.
I ditched the kiddie nametag
and rode to New York
to see the sights and catch
some thrills before contacting Mom.
Manhattan was more than I bargained for.
Amidst crowds and skyscrapers,
I was an ant on the sidewalk.
Scared to tackle the subway,
I never made it uptown.
A social worker spotted me
wandering and could smell
that I was lost. She bought me a meal
and put me up for the night
in what I thought was a fancy hotel
but turned out to be the YWCA.
The next morning, she dropped me off
at the children's home. I stayed there
a couple of weeks until Mrs. Levy,
the lady Mom worked for, picked me up.
We drove to Long Branch, where Mom
had hired me out as a maid.
Harlem would have to wait.

Let's Call the Whole Thing Off

In Long Branch, I worked for a fat lady
who sunned on the beach all day
while I peeled potatoes, washed dishes,
dusted knickknacks, and fluffed pillows.
Fifteen minutes before her husband
came in from work, she shifted
into high gear, giving orders right
and left and calling me "nigger."
No one had called me that before.
Then, one day, she told me to wash
her beach blanket. I said,
I don't do laundry, and told her
where to put her filthy blanket.
She fired me on the spot.
I swore I'd never be a maid again.

Love for Sale

Mom didn't know what to do with me
after I lost my live-in job, but she saw
I wasn't cut out to be a servant.
I was too headstrong, too proud.
Plus, she was tired of scraping by,
and Harlem was calling.

We hit town with little to nothing;
settled uptown in one room
of a high-rent apartment
owned by Florence Williams.
Several women shared the place.
I had been around Alice Dean's
and Ethel Moore's good-time houses
enough to know this was a brothel.
Mom was hired as the housekeeper,
but soon we were both turning tricks.

Harlem was no Promised Land;
it was a sea of black folks, striving
to rise from fields to factories
or from hard luck to street hustles,
flowing through clubs and churches,
grooving on jazz and Jesus.
Harlem was a black sea that parted
each night for white partygoers
with money to burn and cares to shed.
I was swept up by the tide.

Time on My Hands

In late May, the police rounded up
a slew of prostitutes, me and Mom
included, and carted us to jail.
I was fourteen but claimed to be
twenty-one so I wouldn't get shipped off
to reform school. The judge sent me
to Blackwell's Island instead.
I spent six weeks on hospital duty,
giving shots to girls with syphilis,
and one hundred days in the workhouse.
When I wasn't doing laundry
or whipping up meals for the warden,
I was eating food unfit for dogs,
dodging bull dykes and rats
and counting my days till freedom.
By the time I got out in October,
I had lost twenty-three pounds.

Lady's Back in Town

Back on the streets in a flimsy silk dress,
I got a sugar daddy fast, a man to buy me
clothes that fit and a warm winter coat.
Then I got a room in a gambling house
and earned my keep waiting tables
but left after the owner's husband
made a pass at me. When Mom and I
reunited, the Depression was hitting Harlem
right in the gut. Breadlines for blocks.

Do Your Duty

To Clarence's wife, Fanny,
I was a bad seed, a reminder
of his roving eye, his boyhood
mistake, and Mom, a pain
in the neck, carrying a torch
for a man who'd moved on.

Nearly broke, Mom was too proud
to ask Clarence for a cent.
I had no such shame. In my book,
he owed us big. So I asked to live
at his place. There was plenty of room,
but Fanny nixed that plan.

Just One More Chance

By age fifteen, I knew my voice
was my ticket. So I aimed high.
I hit Small's Paradise, itching
to audition. Small's—
where waiters danced the Charleston
balancing trays of drinks,
and well-off whites and blacks
mixed easily as cocktails.
I walked in knowing I was golden.
The piano player asked me
what key I sang in. I shot back,
I don't know, man; just play.
They shooed me out of there
before I could sing one note.
I knew then I had a lot to learn.

I Don't Stand a Ghost of a Chance

During a cold snap, Mom took sick
and couldn't work as a maid.
Rent was past due, and the landlord
threatened to set us out on the street.
We needed cash yesterday.
Refusing to turn tricks again, I pounded
the pavement along Seventh Avenue,
but no one needed kitchen help.
Then I saw a sign in a window:
Dancer Wanted. I couldn't dance
my way out of a box but had to try.
My two left feet shuffled
right into a corner. I was pitiful.
The piano player laughed so hard
he cried. *Honey, you sure can't dance,*
he said. *Can you sing?*
I asked him to play a number
and showed what I could do.
Guests at the tables stopped
chewing and chatting to listen.
When the tune was over,
you could've heard a pin drop.
I landed the job. At last,
I'd get paid to sing my songs:
chicken and waffles plus tips.

You Gotta Show Me

After-hours jam sessions
were a crash course in jazz.
Every chance I got,
I sat beside piano players,
studying their fingers
striding the keyboard,
striking sharps and flats
and major and minor chords,
trilling syncopated melodies.
I trailed their fingers
for octaves as they charmed
the secrets of swing.
Piano masters offered up
music's mysteries.
I put myself in their hands.

Spreadin' the Rhythm Around

Night after night at Mexico's,
Go Grabbers, Club Hot-Cha,
Pod & Jerry's, The Bright Spot,
Alhambra, Shim Sham Club,
or no-name speakeasies,
I spread rhythm like jam
till I grew dizzy from the beat.
For two dollars and tips,
I'd strut from table to table,
singing the same songs
in the same tacky dress,
changing the lyrics slightly
to spice up my act.
I flavored jazz like soul food,
and the night crowd ate it up.

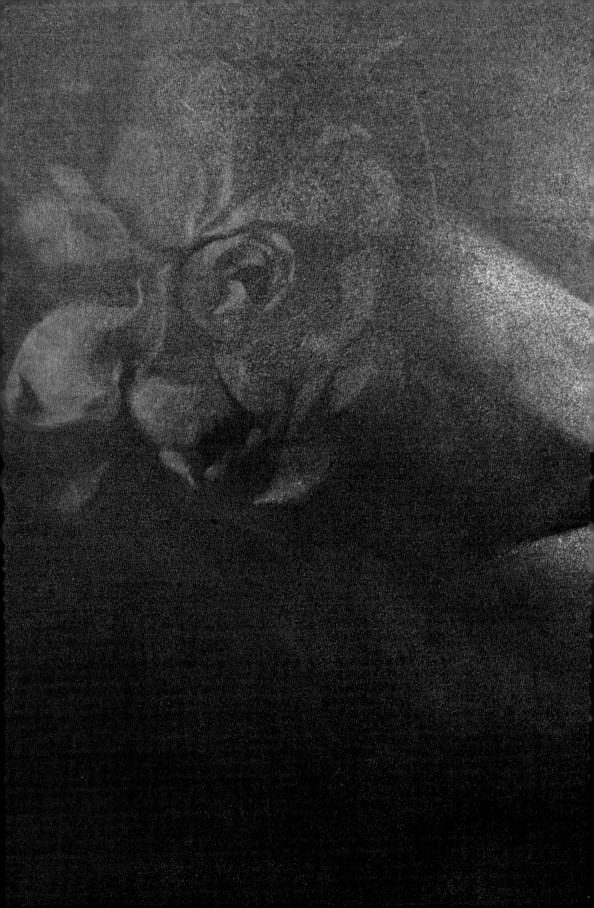

This Is Heaven to Me

Harlem sizzled after dark:
crowded theaters, jumping
dance halls, classy supper clubs,
hole-in-the-wall cafés and taverns,
musty cellars and lounges,
and a rib joint or bar and grill
on every bustling block.
I played more rundown joints
than I can recall; gigs, a blur
of smoke clouds, spotlights,
and struggling musicians like me
with barely a pot to pee in
or a window to throw it out of;
no fame or money yet;
just the thrill of fronting a band
and triggering applause.
That was enough
to put me on cloud nine.

Beyond the Sea (*La Mer*)

I had seen freighters
that docked in Baltimore
between Atlantic crossings,
but I had never felt sand
between my toes.
At Rockaway Beach
with friends, I watched
waves tumble and crash
and sea gulls swoop for trash.
I wore a floral swimsuit
and waded in the surf.

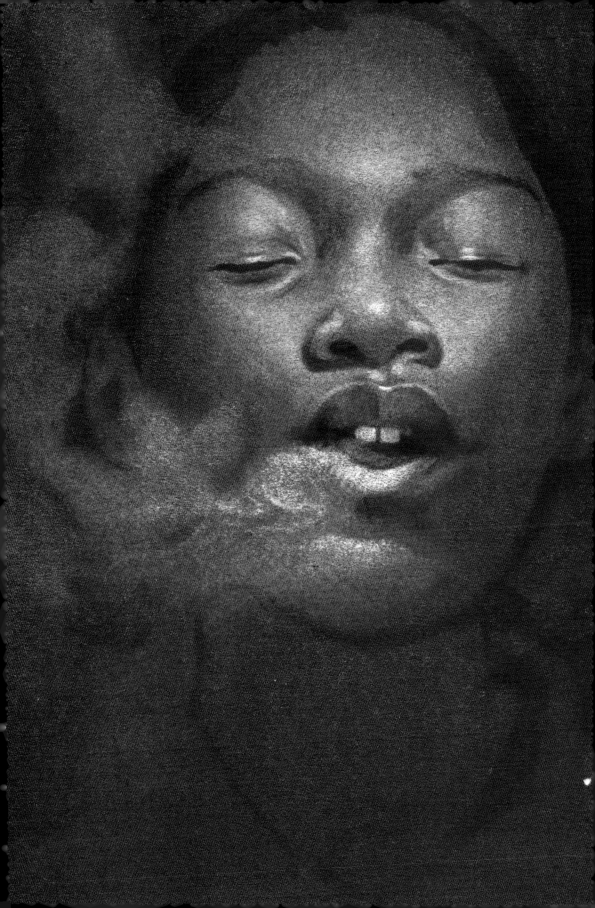

A Fine Romance—

Not once upon a time
or happily ever after;
but the lurid scenes
I savored in salty love comics
and tawdry true confessions.

Titillating headlines whetted my appetite:

Love Letter Romeo
Don't Call Me Darling

In the Looking Glass
I'll Dance Alone

The Day Before Paradise
There Has to Be Moonlight

One Crowded Hour
Her Heart Wore Wings

Saucy plots simmered
to a slow boil, gripping me
in a steamy embrace.

Sure, my tastes
were lowbrow,
but at a dime a serving,
these cheap thrills made
real life seem bland.

Strewn around my bedroom,
piles of pulp fiction—
Love Book, True Story,
Real Tempting Tales,
bonbons I devoured
as midnight snacks.

You Let Me Down

Clarence Holiday played rhythm guitar
for the Fletcher Henderson Orchestra.
In jazz circles, our paths crossed
more often than he liked.
The last thing he wanted
was a buxom girl like me blabbing
that I was his grown-up daughter
and making the good-time gals
think he was an old man.

Once, when rent was due,
I cornered Clarence
at the Roseland Ballroom
and threatened to tell everyone
he was my father if he didn't pay up.
He handed me seven crumpled bills
and told me to scram.
He didn't have to ask twice;
his money cheapened our bond.
Besides, I would've paid
for a chance to call him "Daddy."

Matinee: *American Beauty*

Even though I worked all night and slept
half the day, I still caught matinees sometimes,
especially if Billie Dove was starring.

When she batted her hazel eyes and puckered
her bee-stung lips, there was no doubt
why she was called the American Beauty.

In silent films and talkies, black-and-white
and Technicolor, she blossomed
from damsel in distress to woman of substance.

Between her films, I delved into her private life
through Hollywood gossip magazines—
Picturegoer, Photoplay, Modern Screen.

Born "Lillian," she started young like me.
In a Broadway chorus line at sixteen,
she had the guts to ask for fifty bucks a week.

Then she went from Hollywood bit parts
to leading lady, riding a string of hits
to get top billing at the box office.

As devoted to fans as they were to her,
she signed glamour shots by the thousands.
Love, Billie Dove. What I'd give to own one.

Then she shocked Hollywood when playboy pilot
and movie producer Howard Hughes
paid her husband to divorce her.

Rising above the scandal, Billie ditched
the high-flying Hughes, penned poems,
painted landscapes, and learned to fly herself.

Oh, to wear her wings.

But Not for Me

Introducing: Eleanora Fagan,
Eleanora and Her Esquires,
Eleanora and the Encore Orchestra,
Nora and the New Yorkers.
All wrong.

Eleanora Fagan was fine
for some bawdy barmaid
or factory worker right off the boat,
fine for a striving domestic
fresh from the cotton fields,
but not for a blues mama,
not for me.

Eleanora Fagan had vaudeville
written all over it.
I needed a name to carry me
from Harlem to Hollywood,
to spark applause when emcees
called me onstage;
a name to light marquees.

Bessie Smith was the empress;
Mamie Smith, the queen;
titles earned by record sales.
And I was an unknown.
Eleanora who?

I needed a name that fit like a silk gown,
a name to drape like a pearl mink stole
across my shoulders.

My daddy Clarence rarely gave me
the time of day, so I took
what I wanted—a hint of his name.

The movie star Billie Dove, my idol,
supplied the other half—a name
equal parts tomboy and flirt.

Billie Halliday.
Miss Billie Halliday.
Now, that has an uptown ring.

I Can't Believe That You're in Love with Me

One night at Brownies, Bobby Henderson
sat in for my piano player Dot Hill.
He'd play a few bars and I'd say,
Do that again. What you just did.
He peered up from the keyboard at me,
and I saw a woman in his eyes.
He couldn't believe I was just sixteen.
That night, we floated from club to club—
Bobby on stride piano and me
at the mic—until we had landed a gig.

Nights in the spotlight and in the glare
of day, our flirtation was a long song.
Mornings, Bobby fixed breakfast
at his mother's place and watched me eat
as if dining were an exotic dance.
Dainty, he called me. *Dainty.*
When I invited him to meet Mom,
she tried dragging him into our tiffs,
but Bobby wouldn't take sides.
We'd talk for hours; I'd laugh till I shook.

Sweet as cotton candy, he yearned
to ease my fears, though
I never let on what was aching me.
When I lashed out at folks
who'd done me wrong,
Bobby stood by me like a tree.
For a year or more, we played
the bar-and-grill circuit like a melody.
Everyone thought we'd get married.
I sure missed our music when we split.

How Deep Is the Ocean?

Without the microphone,
there would be no spotlight,
no band backing me
with bluesy swing.

My voice was small,
barely an octave,
but the mic enlarged my songs,
let me hold listeners close.

With the microphone,
my voice was an ocean,
deep as my moods,
and audiences dove in.

Too Marvelous for Words

From where I stood, unknown
beyond these neon-lit streets,
Monette Moore had arrived.
She had done Broadway
and had her own supper club by 1933.
At eighteen, I was hired to sing
so the hostess could greet her guests.

John Hammond, a young white guy
who dropped out of Yale to produce
records, had slummed uptown
to scout Monette, but he stumbled
upon me instead. Singing slightly
behind the beat, mouthing each phrase
just so, I knocked John's socks off.
He came back every night, dragging
up-and-coming bandleaders
like Benny Goodman and Count Basie
to see me. I was the kind
of find John dreamed of.
He wasn't as square as I thought.

John wrote me up in *Melody Maker,*
a British newspaper, and raved
that I was the best jazz singer ever.
After three short weeks,
Monette's place closed,
but a door had opened for me.

Everything I Have Is Yours

The ring off my finger
or the roof over my head,
a place to hang your hat
and lay your tired bones,
my next meal or last dollar.
Nothing's too good for a friend.

That's Life I Guess

My daddy never had
room for me in his heart.
But for a few magic nights,
I was at the mic
while Clarence strummed strings
with Harlem's hottest band;
close as we'd come to harmony.
That gig hit a sour note
the second his wife found out.
She had me fired.

Please Don't Talk About Me When I'm Gone

Ethel Waters came up
the hard way like me—
but in the Philly slums.
A sixth-grade dropout,
she married at thirteen
and divorced after one year
as a punching bag
for a no-good man.

She might have worked
as a maid forever
if two vaudeville producers
hadn't heard her singing
at a talent contest.
On the chittlin' circuit,
they billed her
as Sweet Mama String Bean.
She was cutting records
when I was still playing tag.

No shouter or growler
like most blues mamas,
Ethel sang low and sweet,
her voice smoldering,
mouthing each word
as if a secret song
about her private pain.

She shimmied her way
into many a heart
but pierced mine with a jibe.
The day I cut my first record,
she sat in the studio sneering,
*She sings like her shoes
are two sizes too small.*

I could have put my foot
right up her behind.

Pennies from Heaven

On borrowed time in a studio booked
for Ethel Waters, I was scared stiff.
I had never heard my own voice
and wasn't sure I wanted to.

I cleared my throat a few times,
rubbed my clammy palms on my skirt,
and tapped my foot timidly to the beat.
The piano player sensed I was stalling.

Don't be a square, he said.
Just close your eyes and sing.
I shut out everything but the music.
Before I knew it, the session was over.

My first record, a 78 with Benny Goodman,
had "Riffin' the Scotch" on one side
and "My Mother's Son-in-Law" on the other,
tunes no first-rate singer would have sung.

I didn't care about the selections.
I earned thirty-five bucks, no royalties back then.
The record went nowhere fast,
but my swinging ride had begun.

When You're Smiling

Still strapped for cash, I joined
a song and dance act
at Pod & Jerry's Log Cabin.
First, hoofer Honi Coles tapped onstage,
and then Baby Lawrence sang.
He was eleven and I loved him to death.
High Jivin' Smiley cracked half-baked jokes,
and I closed each show.
On good nights, we'd split
ten to twenty bucks in tips.
I always went home smiling.

Our Love Is Different

Mom would have liked
to keep me on a shorter leash.
Still, no matter how late
I stayed out, no matter where I was
or who I was with, I called
home to ease her mind.

Mom wouldn't hear
of my boyfriends sleeping over
but never said a word when I brought
girls home: prostitutes, socialites,
and stars. I won't drop names,
but I had them call me "Bill."

Just Friends

Lester Young had five years on me,
but I hit Harlem first. He came
by way of the Mississippi Delta
and Minneapolis and played tenor sax
for the Fletcher Henderson Orchestra.
Lester knew music inside out
but didn't know beans about New York.
Poor thing slept with one eye open
after a rat pounced on him in a cheap hotel.
The dark circles rimming his green eyes
said it all. Lester was practically a stray.
I offered him the spare room in the flat
I shared with Mom, and Lester leaped
into our lives. We loved him beyond words.
With his oddball ways, jive-talking
riddles, and silly superstitions, Lester
tickled me and mellowed Mom.
He gave us nicknames that stuck for life:
Mom was the Duchess and I was Lady Day.
I called him "Prez," short for the President.
He became the brother that I never had.

I Get a Kick Out Of You

Whenever he could, Lester sat in
with me at bar and grills.
We were carefree night birds
flying behind the beat,
winging our way through blue notes
as slowly as we pleased.
Our duets, conversations
between twin souls,
were perfect musical pairings.
Prez played sax like a singer
and I thought like a horn.
We took turns swinging solos
that spun ballads into gold.

Body and Soul

Something holy happened
when Prez and I played.
We were spirits dwelling
within the same heart.
Prez's horn held me
like a father's loving arms.

Nice Work If You Can Get It

I sang all hours of the night
but had days free.
So my songwriter friend Sidney
urged me to try acting,
first on radio soap operas.
Sidney must have sensed
I had a flair for drama.

He got my foot in the door
and I doubled as wife and maid
on the same show.
With plots that crept
at a snail's pace, one lovers' tiff
dragged on for weeks.

At fifteen dollars a day,
I pocketed a chunk of change
by the time they kissed and made up.
Not bad for moonlighting.

Matinee: *Emperor Jones*

Not a leading lady,
not a supporting player,
not even a bit part—
an extra—
but in Paul Robeson's shadow
just the same.

He had already made a name
for himself as a stage actor,
concert singer, and all-American athlete.
He even went to law school—Columbia.
To me, he was a god.

With a booming baritone
and regal bearing,
he headlined an all-black cast,
taking *Emperor Jones*
from Broadway to the big screen,
filming on Long Island, not in Hollywood.

Robeson played Brutus Jones,
who rose from Pullman porter, swindler,
murderer, and convict to Caribbean warlord—
a climb summed up in one line:
I betcha they knows a man when they sees one.
Of course, he met a tragic end.

The role made Paul Robeson
the first black movie star.
He had more black power
in his voice than most men
have in their whole bodies.
I sure was tickled to be a face in the crowd.

It's Like Reaching for the Moon

The Apollo Theater hadn't been open long,
but the Tree of Hope was a Harlem tradition
with entertainers hungry for their big break.
When the tree stood on Seventh Avenue,
show biz hopefuls touched it for good luck.
After the tree was cut down to widen the street,
its logs sold as souvenirs and a slice of the trunk
went to the Apollo Theater, a proving ground
for budding black artists. Before their acts,
performers stroked the tree trunk. Then they reached
toward spotlights like branches beneath the moon.
After chugging along on the bar-and-grill
circuit, I debuted at the Apollo in 1934.
I'd outgrown superstitions, but I kissed
the trunk and prayed, hoping not to get booed.

I Can't Face the Music

I was backstage when the big band played.
I had never sung for more than two hundred,
and two thousand people had paid
the twenty-five-cents admission that day.
Apollo audiences were tough customers
that could make or break careers.
In the wings, my knees were knocking.

When my cue came up, I froze in fear.
Comedian "Pigmeat" Markham shoved me onstage.
I might have fallen if not for the microphone stand.
A haze of smoke filtered the spotlight. I opened
with "If the Moon Turns Green" and closed
with an encore. Tore that packed house down.

Twenty-Four Hours a Day

With Clare, Carmen, and Mae,
singers like me with big dreams
who were more like sisters than friends,
life was a nonstop party.
We'd sing all night and then
prowl the clubs: the Silver Dollar,
Brown Bomber, and my favorite,
Jimmy's Chicken Shack.
When they closed, we'd head
to the gin mills or reefer pads;
a chorus of light-headed laughter.
I'd go to bed at 4:00 or 5:00 p.m., sleep,
and go back to work at 2:00 a.m.—
seven days a week, no nights off—
and never miss a beat.

Sophisticated Lady

John Hammond dubbed me
a star on the rise.
So impresario Irving Mills
tapped me for a movie role,
with Duke Ellington no less.

The suave bandleader-composer
was the toast of Harlem,
holding sway in black tie and tails
at New York's swankiest night spot,
the whites-only Cotton Club.

Black waiters and performers catered
to well-heeled guests slumming uptown.
They swung the night away to hot jazz
and dazzling revues in lush cabarets.
The rest of us listened on radios.

We answered Duke's "Creole Love Call,"
glimpsed his "Black and Tan Fantasy,"
felt his "Mood Indigo," and heeded
his hip decree: "It Don't Mean a Thing
If It Ain't Got That Swing."

In true Duke fashion, the production
we were filming had a la-de-da title—
Symphony in Black: A Rhapsody of Negro Life—
and four parts: "The Laborers," "A Triangle,"
"A Hymn of Sorrow," and "Harlem Rhythm."

Duke gave singers sound advice—
Slip on a stage persona and stick with it.
He shaped his music to each singer's mold.
The film's only vocal, a number
called "Blues," fit me like a second skin.

I played a gal jilted by a two-timing man.
To the wailing of an oboe, he knocked me
to the floor—seventy times in as many takes—
till I was black-and-blue. As a muted trumpet
wept, I sang my number from the ground.

The whole *Symphony* was less than
ten minutes long, but that didn't matter
to Mom. She bragged all over Harlem
that I was bound to be a star, prodded
all her friends to watch for the premiere.

I'm in a Low Down Groove

I lived in the blues the way
some people did a house.
Sometimes, I'd stay in
for days without opening
the door for a blessed soul.
My own sad company
was all I cared to keep.

Gimme a Pigfoot and a Bottle of Beer

Mom was all into my business,
warning me about choices in men,
scolding me about staying out too late,
reminding me of her mistakes over
and over again, as if I too was doomed.
She'd been abandoned by her father,
dumped by my father, divorced
by her husband, and ditched
by her live-in lover. Mom clung to me
like I was a doll, fearing I'd leave
if she let go. Yet the squabbling
drove me away. I pitied her.
Once the money was rolling in
from recording sessions,
I rented an apartment at 99th Street
and Central Park West and set
Mom up in a soul food restaurant.
She could put a hurtin' on spareribs
but was bighearted like me
and had no head for business,
feeding any sack with a sob story.
I didn't care if she ever broke even.
Money was easy come, easy go.
As long as Mom kept busy in the kitchen,
I could stay out of the frying pan.

I Only Have Eyes for You

I guess I'm a sucker
for a sad-eyed pooch
'cause I was a stray myself,
running the streets, going from pillar
to post as a girl, not sure when
or where Mom would pawn me off
on neighbors or distant kin.

Someday when I settle down,
I'm gonna get a dog to wag its tail
like a metronome when I come home
and nudge me with its nose.
I'll take my pooch everywhere—
clubs, restaurants, even church—
and dare a soul to throw us out.

That's All I Ask of You

Clarence got wind of the gossip:
That torch singer
Billie Halliday is copying
Louis Armstrong's style
instead of finding her own.
In the spring of 1935, Clarence
dropped by Club Hot-Cha
to catch my show, hear for himself.
When I took my bow, he raised
a glass to me and winked.
He knew I wasn't anyone's copy;
I was an original,
making a name for myself.
And, for once, he was proud.
I longed to hug him,
but when I reached his table,
he had gone. I changed my name
again—to Holiday this time.

Them There Eyes

My brows were pencil thin,
not because that was the fashion
but because while trying to shape them,
I shaved one halfway off.
To save face, I drew a perfect arch
and smudged my lids before the show.
Onstage, shadowy eyes shut,
I peered inside the melody,
peeked behind the rhythm,
and sang what the song meant.

I'm a Fool to Want You

A tenor sax man with a dark side,
Ben Webster came out slugging
after a few drinks. I fell
for him hard, and his fist
left my face black-and-blue.
I don't know what I saw in him,
but Mom was fighting mad
when she saw my bruises.
Ben came by our place and she
whacked him with an umbrella.
Ben was bad news
that I was slow to read.

I Got It Bad (and That Ain't Good)

While my heart healed, I
pinned gardenias in my hair
to hide the bruises.

These 'N' That 'N' Those

The room I called my playroom held
a record player and an old upright piano.
My record collection went from soup to nuts.
I'd just as soon boogie to Fats Waller's
Harlem anthem "Ain't Misbehavin'"
as soak in a tub full of bubbles
to Debussy's "Afternoon of a Faun"
or Ravel's red-hot "Bolero."
But those two French dudes couldn't hold
a candle to Brooklyn's George Gershwin.
Overlooking Central Park, I knitted
to his *Porgy and Bess* and stirred coffee
to *Rhapsody in Blue*. On my turntable,
I gave all sorts of music a spin.

Now They Call It Swing

Between 5th and 6th avenues, 52nd Street
never slept. It was the new scene, musicians'
hangouts-turned-hot-spots, where jazz miracles
played out every night. They called it Swing Street.
My first gig there, at the Famous Door, lasted
only two weeks, but that was long enough
to see this wasn't Harlem anymore.
The Famous Door did not allow mixing
between black talent and white customers.
I stewed between sets in the upstairs hall,
letting the slight sink in. But when I walked
onstage, I glided into the spotlight
with my head above the crowd.
The next year, I played the Onyx Club.
The hoity-toity crowd didn't dig me.
But I soon won them and conquered
Swing Street, too.

Things Are Looking Up

At twenty-one, I had cut as many sides
with bandleaders like Benny Goodman
and Teddy Wilson, but not one song
under my own name. Still, the records sold.
By July 1936, I had gained enough steam
to headline a session, front my own band—
a changing crew of musicians any given week—
Billie Holiday and Her Orchestra performing
"Billie's Blues," "Did I Remember?," "No Regrets,"
and Gershwin's "Summertime."
Bubbling with jazz, I never looked back.

I've Got a Date with a Dream

My first gig outside New York;
Montreal might as well have been Paris.
I couldn't speak a lick of French
but loved hearing it, especially how it
rolled off Jean-Louis's tongue. *Je t'adore,*
he said as he toasted me with champagne.
I took my first taste and didn't care for it,
but I did care for him. I'll never know
what might have been if his folks
had not found out and nipped us in the bud.
Before I left the city, Jean-Louis left a rose
along with a note addressed *Ma Cherie.*

Detour Ahead

Touring with Count Basie
meant headlining at hotels
where we couldn't sleep
and playing one-nighters
at juke joints and dance halls
where some drunken fool might knife
a man over a two-timing woman.

Playing with Basie's big band
meant riding a Blue Goose bus
all day and night,
passing Vacancy signs
aimed at whites only
till we reached a black hotel
or rooming house where we could
rest our tired bones.

Traveling with Daddy Basie
meant being the only girl
among sixteen guys,
learning to shoot craps
from old hands and then
kneeling with Lady Luck
till I wore holes in my hose
and beat those boys
at their own game.

Being part of Basie's band
meant cutting up with Prez,
treating the fellas to my home cooking,
and, when they gambled their pay away,
coming to their rescue with loans
for sweethearts' Christmas gifts.

Working for the Count
meant being shorted on payday,
not having cash for a hot dog,
and never having the right clothes,
equipment, or instruments
but always having the right sound.

Swinging with Basie's band
meant barely being able to read
a note between us, yet knowing
a hundred songs by heart;
seventeen musicians playing
by ear and breathing as one.
Count Basie's big band
was the jazziest party on wheels.

Do You Know What It Means to Miss New Orleans?

Say what you will about the South:
the worst racist I came up against
was not deep down in Dixie
but way up in Detroit with Basie's band.
The boss at the Fox Theater claimed
I was too high yellow,
too light-skinned, to share
the stage with black musicians
and might be mistaken for white.
The one condition for the show to go on:
that I darken my skin with greasepaint.
I smiled to keep from throwing up
and never missed Harlem more.

Foolin' Myself

I went on tour to see America
and send money home for a nest egg.
That plan flew out the window
of a Blue Goose bus, went the way
of wardrobe and hairdo expenses,
restaurant checks and hotel bills
that barely left cash for a stamp.
I sent Mom postcards instead of savings.
But I wouldn't trade that time—
not for a million bucks.

One for My Baby (and One More for the Road)

Before I went on tour
with Artie Shaw's band, Mom
gave me a big send-off:
a home-cooked breakfast
for sixteen fellas and me.
They ate her fried chicken
like it was going out of style
and said they'd never tasted
angel biscuits so divine.
It would be a month of Sundays
before they did again.

Moonlight in Vermont

Artie hit it big with "Begin the Beguine"
and bought himself a Rolls-Royce—
a car fit for the King of England
but not the new King of Swing, not a band
on a mad dash through New England
to play a prep-school prom. The ride
was smooth as long as we cruised,
but that Rolls rumbled like a jackhammer
when Artie gave it the gas.
My insides were scrambled eggs
when we reached Massachusetts.
I was relieved when the headmaster
said I couldn't go onstage. Helen Forrest,
the white singer Artie hired to play
theaters that wouldn't let a black singer
onstage with a white band,
thought she'd get a chance to shine—
but no such luck. The headmaster
didn't let any gals on his stage.
I caught some Z's and let poor Helen stew.

Please Don't Do It in Here

When a fly buzzed through
Artie's car, I nearly flew
right out the window.

I Don't Know If I'm Coming or Going

Artie Shaw broke new ground
tapping me for his all-white band.
As we went West, the color line
was plain as the stripe down a highway,
and the fellas pressed me to cross it.
When hotel managers shut me out
or a redneck called me "nigger"
or a theater owner said I'd go onstage
over his dead body, my bandmates
took it personal. If they didn't storm out,
they came to blows with bigots.
The battles over closed doors wore on me.
So I ate and slept apart from the band
and peed in a cup or in the bushes
while my bandmates used restrooms.
Artie finally bowed to the pressure
and had Helen perform in my place down South.
He asked me to help her with phrasing.
I didn't mind, but she resented me.
At least, there was another girl in the band.

That scene played out again in New York.
A hotel manager wouldn't let me sit onstage
between vocal numbers as Artie asked,
so I was stuck in a suite half the show
and rode down on cue by freight elevator.
The band had too much riding on that show
to fight a New York hotel and a network.
And I couldn't lose my chance
to be broadcast live on radio.
Besides, fans who tuned in couldn't see
where I was sitting and Mom,
bless her heart, listened every single night.
After a couple of weeks, the show's sponsor,
Old Gold cigarettes, ordered Artie
to sack the colored singer or else.
That gig was grossing twenty-five grand a week,
and the band was forced to let me go.

With Thee I Swing

Racism ripped America at the seams,
and jazz stitched the nation together
one song at a time. But music
alone couldn't mend the tear.
The needle pricked my fingers
till my soul was sore, and I longed
to hop a train for home.

Big Stuff

After touring, my bookings dried up.
I returned to Harlem clubs
but longed to headline again.
I laid down the law, threatened
to ax my manager if he didn't get
me some gigs. Then he lowered
the boom, told me I was fat.
Greasing on soul food
had pushed me past two hundred.
I shed some extra weight
but kept my curves and voice.
At Chicago's Grand Terrace Club,
I was in fine form.

The Way You Look Tonight

Off and on, Mom hit the road
as my dresser, zipping my gowns
and pinning flowers in my hair.
Backstage, we were like sisters.
She prayed I'd make it big.

You Turned the Tables on Me

When I wasn't working,
I'd go to a little East Side joint
to catch Mabel Mercer's show.
She was born in England
and had been the toast of Paris
when *le jazz hot* reached a boil.
She had a way with phrasing
and knew how to choose a song.
For my money, Mabel
owned the cabaret scene.
I could listen to her all night.

I Gotta Right to Sing the Blues

No one taught me to sing just behind the beat,
to tease listeners with my tempo,
to glide above the band, flit between
musicians like a canary finally free.
No one trained me to blow like a horn,
to milk a measure by bending the melody,
to breathe a universe in a single note,
and end a song in a different key.
No one told me to bridge sound and feeling,
to be a statue in the spotlight, gesturing
with a nod of my head or wave of my hand,
to stand my ground and never bow.
That came natural, baby. That all came natural.

I Cried for You

Clarence was touring with a band
when a cold turned to pneumonia
that he tried to drown with drink.
When he reached a veterans' hospital,
it was too late. The phone call
came for me from Dallas.
My daddy took his last breath
on February 23, 1937.
Clarence's closing act,
his funeral, was a farce
with three women vying
to play the widow.
His wife, Fanny, his mistress Atlanta,
and two out-of-wedlock children
so light they could pass for white
sat teary-eyed at the gravesite.
Too ornery to ride with Fanny,
Mom rented a Cadillac, got lost,
and arrived after the benediction.
Any hope I had of knowing
a father's love was buried
six feet down.

If Dreams Come True

I will bathe in spotlights
and sleep on satin.
Gardenias will bloom
year-round in my backyard.
Sadie's rib joint will make
rich folks lick their fingers.
Prez and I will do ten dozen duets.
Crooners will sing my praises
between the lines of songs.
Horn men will trumpet my arrival
and claim me as their own.
Piano players will secretly
pine for me as my solos
move them to tears.
Singers will try but fail
to mimic my tempo and phrasing.
My biography will light
the silver screen; my myth,
inseparable from my music.
Cats will groove to my blues
long after I'm gone,
a legacy in wax.
History will hail me
in the same breath as Duke
and Count—jazz royalty.
I will reign over Swing Street
and have found the love I crave.

Coda: Strange Fruit

After years of being barred
from entering front doors,
sitting on bandstands,
and mingling at whites-only clubs,
how could I not headline
Café Society, one of the first joints
to let blacks and whites mix?

After being called "nigger wench"
down South and "high yellow"
in Detroit, how could I resist
the chance to sing in my own skin?

After a cigarette sponsor cut me
from its radio show, how could I not
yearn to again breathe free?

After moving from place to place
to place as a child, how could I not
relish a long run in Greenwich Village,
New York's hippest haunt?

How could I not thrive
at a place where the owner,
an ex–shoe salesman, worshipped
the ground I walked on,
and waiters asked noisy patrons to leave
rather than disturb my show?

When the NAACP hung the flag
A MAN WAS LYNCHED YESTERDAY
from its 69th Street office,
how could I not long to voice outrage?

When schoolteacher Lewis Allan
showed me his protest poem
about a lynching and plucked
a somber melody on the piano,
how could I let that tune slip away
without passing through my lips?

When the waiters stopped service,
the room was pitch black
except for a spotlight on my face,
and I stood completely still,
performing "Strange Fruit,"
how could I not shed tears?

When I arrived at Café Society
a girl singer with a string of hits
and departed the star of the hour,
how could I not claim:
This is my song?

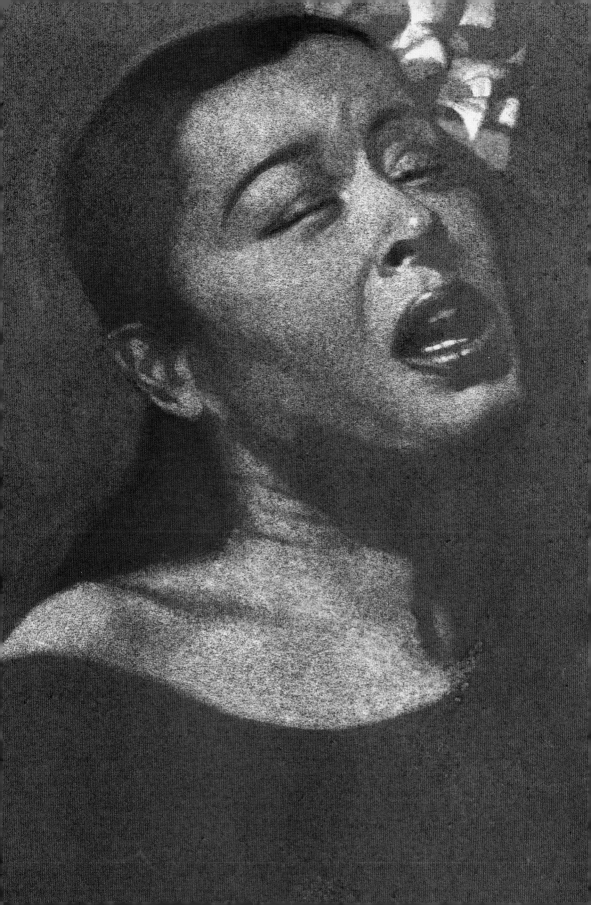

AFTERWORD

Billie Holiday may have been my muse even before I was a poet. Thanks to my father's musical tastes, jazz was the soundtrack of my preschool years. His record collection included the great ladies of jazz: Ella Fitzgerald, Sarah Vaughan, Dinah Washington, and, yes, Billie Holiday. The first Billie Holiday album that I ever heard was her last major recording, *Lady in Satin*. I could sing "You've Changed" as well as any nursery song. I was just three years old when the legendary vocalist died in 1959. In the decade that followed, the sounds of the sixties—rock and rhythm and blues—took me on a detour from jazz.

The 1972 film *Lady Sings the Blues* was my road back—to jazz and to Billie. The melodramatic biopic sealed my devotion to Lady Day. I could not get enough of her soul-stirring voice. I collected one Billie Holiday recording after another. Her heartrending life story—her troubled childhood in my hometown of Baltimore, her rise in Harlem to jazz royalty, her hard luck with love, her run-ins with racists and the law, and her decline caused by alcoholism and drug addiction—also struck a chord.

Were it not for music, the girl who grew up Eleanora Fagan certainly would not have become Billie Holiday. With a limited vocal range but vast emotive capability, her voice is a marvel. For weeks before I wrote a single poem, I listened to Billie's early recordings and let them speak to me. In those songs, I found a young songbird, bubbling with joy over jazz she clearly dug. I realized then that Lady was not singing the blues; she was singing her life. Thus, I decided that this fictional verse memoir would unfold through first-person poems titled after her songs. And I chose to end on a high note as twenty-five-year-old Lady Day, in full bloom with gardenias in her hair, sings "Strange Fruit," the song that became her signature.

Combining oral histories from Billie Holiday's contemporaries with the myth she honed in her sensationalized autobiography, this verse memoir imagines her legendary life from birth to young adulthood. By then, she had virtually raised herself, suffered a rape, done time in reform school and jail, drunk bootleg liquor, smoked then-legal marijuana, appeared in films with Duke Ellington and Paul Robeson, recorded a string of hits, and become the first African American vocalist to tour with an all-white band. The young woman who speaks through these poems is Billie Holiday before heroin and hard living took their toll.

If I could sing, I might not write. Writing poetry is as close as I come to making music. Oh, I do groove to female jazz vocalists—Madeleine Peyroux, Diane Reeves, Cassandra Wilson, Nnenna Freelon, and Lady Day—on my commute to work. My dream Billie Holiday CD would definitely include these faves:

"Getting Some Fun Out Of Life"
"Can't Help Lovin' Dat Man"
"Summertime"
"Love Me or Leave Me"
"God Bless the Child"
"Autumn in New York"
"Moonlight in Vermont"
"Ain't Nobody's Business If I Do"
"I Gotta Right to Sing the Blues"
"Strange Fruit"

BIOGRAPHIES

Lewis Allan (1903–1986)—Abel Meeropol, a Jewish schoolteacher and union activist from the Bronx, New York, adopted "Lewis Allan" as his pen name. In the late 1930s, Allan wrote the haunting song "Strange Fruit" in response to a photograph of a lynching. In 1939, Billie Holiday recorded the song and it became her most famous.

Louis Armstrong (1901–1971)—A native of New Orleans, Louisiana, cornet player and gravely voiced singer Louis "Satchmo" Armstrong was one of the world's greatest jazz musicians. As a child, Billie Holiday listened to Armstrong's records, and she later appeared with him in the film *New Orleans*.

William "Count" Basie (1904–1984)—Born in Red Bank, New Jersey, Basie toured as a soloist and music director before getting stranded in Kansas City in 1927. There, he played for silent movie theaters and formed his own band. Radio broadcasts propelled the Count Basie Orchestra into one of the leading big bands of the Swing Era.

Charles "Honi" Coles (1911–1992)—Philadelphia-born Coles was a self-taught tap dancer who performed first on the streets of his hometown, then in Harlem clubs and theaters and eventually on Broadway.

Billie Dove (1903–1997)—Born Lilian Bohny, Dove aspired to a film career at an early age. She played bit parts until her performance in the Ziegfeld Follies on Broadway led to leading-lady roles in silent films and early talkies. Dubbed the "American Beauty," Dove retired from Hollywood in 1933.

Edward "Duke" Ellington (1899–1974)—A native of Washington, D.C., Ellington and his orchestra became famous during a long run at the Cotton Club in the 1920s. In a fifty-year career as pianist, bandleader, and composer, he wrote and recorded hundreds of compositions and played in more than twenty thousand performances around the world. Best known for his jazz compositions, Ellington also wrote classical and sacred music.

Benny Goodman (1909–1986)—Chicago-born Goodman played the clarinet and led a big band that rose to fame during the Swing Era of the 1930s. Billie Holiday first recorded with Goodman's band.

Sarah Harris Fagan Gough (1896–1945)—Born out of wedlock in Baltimore, Maryland, Sarah, nicknamed "Sadie," was still a teenager when she gave birth to Billie Holiday in 1915. Sadie never wed Billie's father, Clarence Holiday, but was briefly married to longshoreman Philip Gough. As a child, Billie was often left in the care of relatives or neighbors while Sadie worked elsewhere as a live-in maid. On a few occasions, Sadie ran her own soul-food restaurants.

John Hammond (1910–1987)—A member of a wealthy New York family, Hammond discovered some of the biggest musical talents of the twentieth century, including Benny Goodman, Billie Holiday, Count Basie, Bob Dylan, Aretha Franklin, and Bruce Springsteen. A producer, writer, critic, and an NAACP board member, Hammond helped integrate the music business.

Fletcher Henderson (1898–1952)—Born in Cuthbert, Georgia, Henderson led the most commercially successful African American jazz band of the 1920s. His orchestra's smooth sound gave birth to the 1930s Swing Era. Clarence Holiday, Billie's father, played guitar with Henderson's band.

Clarence Holiday (1898–1937)—A Baltimore-born musician, Clarence Holiday, Billie's father, never lived with and rarely visited Billie and her mother, Sadie. He played banjo before becoming a rhythm guitarist in New York, where he played with the Fletcher Henderson Orchestra.

Howard Hughes (1905–1976)—A native of Humble, Texas, Hughes inherited a family fortune as a teen and became an aviator, engineer, industrialist, and a film producer. Known as a Hollywood playboy and record-setting pilot, Hughes was one of the wealthiest men in the world.

Carmen McRae (1920–1994)—A Harlem native, McRae studied classical piano as a child and became a jazz vocalist, musician, and songwriter. Influenced early on by her friend Billie Holiday, McRae was also known for singing behind the beat.

Mabel Mercer (1900–1984)—Born in Staffordshire, England, Mercer toured Europe in vaudeville and music hall engagements with her aunt before becoming a supper club and cabaret performer in Paris, France, and the United States. She was known for her unique vocal style that told stories through song.

Paul Robeson (1898–1976)—Born in Princeton, New Jersey, Robeson, the son of an ex-slave, was a twentieth-century Renaissance man who distinguished himself as an athlete, a scholar, performer, and political activist. An actor and a singer, Robeson starred on Broadway and in films. During the Communist scare that swept the U.S. Congress in the 1940s, Robeson's passport was revoked because of his black nationalist and anticolonialist views. Although Robeson's passport was eventually reinstated, his career never recovered.

Artie Shaw (1910–2004)—Born Arthur Jacob Arshawsky in New Rochelle, New York, and raised in New Haven, Connecticut, jazz clarinetist and bandleader Shaw became known as the new "King of Swing" after his 1938 hit record "Begin the Beguine." Shaw broke new ground by tapping Billie Holiday as vocalist for his all-white band.

Bessie Smith (1898–1937)—Born in Chattanooga, Tennessee, Smith went from a street musician and minstrel-show performer to become the greatest classic blues singer and top-selling African American recording artist of the 1920s.

Mamie Smith (1883–1946)—Born in Cincinnati, Ohio, Smith was the first person to record blues songs, in 1920. Her second record, "Crazy Blues," sold more than one million copies in one year and opened the door of the recording industry for other African American artists. A singer, piano player, and, later, an actress, Smith influenced every classic blues singer of the 1920s.

Ben Webster (1909–1973)—A native of Kansas City, Missouri, Webster—along with Lester Young and Coleman Hawkins—was one of the most influential tenor saxophonists of the Swing Era. In 1940, he became the first major tenor soloist of Duke Ellington's orchestra.

Teddy Wilson (1912–1986)—Born Theodore Shaw, Wilson studied music at Talladega College before working with Louis Armstrong and others in Chicago. Wilson moved to New York in 1933, where he accompanied Billie Holiday on several recording sessions and played piano for Benny Goodman's trio, becoming one of the first African American musicians featured with white bands.

Lester "Prez" Young (1909–1959)—Raised in a musical family in New Orleans and Minneapolis, tenor saxophonist Young joined Count Basie's band in Kansas City, Missouri. Known for melodic improvisation, Young is remembered for his recordings with Basie and with Billie Holiday.

REFERENCES

Blackburn, Julia. *With Billie*. New York: Pantheon, 2005.

Clarke, Donald. *Wishing on the Moon: The Life and Times of Billie Holiday*. New York: Viking, 1994.

CMG Worldwide. Billie Holiday: The Official Site of Lady Day. www.cmgworldwide.com/music/holiday.*

Document Records. *Symphony in Black (A Rhapsody of Negro Life)*. www.redhotjazz.com/sib.html.

Gottlieb, William P. *The Golden Age of Jazz: Text and Photographs*. San Francisco: Pomegranate Artbooks, 1995.

Griffin, Farah Jasmine. *If You Can't Be Free, Be a Mystery: In Search of Billie Holiday*. New York: Free Press, 2001.

Holiday, Billie. *Lady Day: The Complete Billie Holiday on Columbia (1933–1944)*. Sony, CXK 85470. Ⓟ 2001 by Sony (10 discs).

Holiday, Billie. *Lady Sings the Blues*. With William Duffy. New York: Penguin, 1992.

Jazz Rhythm / Dave Radlauer. "Lester Young." www.jazzhot.bigstep.com/generic.html?pid=10.

Kempton, Arthur. "Street Diva." *New York Review of Books*, July 14, 2005. www.nybooks.com/articles/18114.

Nicholson, Stuart. *Billie Holiday*. Boston: Northeastern University Press, 1995.

Public Broadcasting Service. *Jazz: A Film by Ken Burns*. www.pbs.org/jazz.

University of Michigan School of Information, Cultural Heritage Initiative for Community Outreach. Harlem, 1900–1940: An African American Community. An Exhibition Portfolio from the Schomburg Center for Research in Black Culture, New York Public Library. www.si.umich.edu/chico/Harlem/index.html.

Ward, Geoffrey. *Jazz: A History of America's Music*. New York: Alfred A. Knopf, 2000.

Williams, Martin. *The Jazz Tradition*. 2nd rev. ed. New York: Oxford University Press, 1993.

FURTHER READING AND LISTENING

Gourse, Leslie. *Billie Holiday: The Tragedy and Triumph of Lady Day*. New York: Franklin Watts, 1995.

Greene, Meg. *Billie Holiday: A Biography*. Westport, CT: Greenwood Press, 2007.

Holiday, Billie. *The Best of Billie Holiday: The Millennium Collection; 20th Century Masters*. Verve, 3145899952. Ⓟ 2002 by Verve.

Holiday, Billie. *Ken Burns Jazz: Definitive Billie Holiday*. Verve, 3145490812. Ⓟ 2000 by Verve.

Kliment, Bud. *Billie Holiday*. New York: Chelsea House, 1990.

* All Web sites active at time of publication

Floyd Cooper's art for this book was created with a subtractive technique, using erasers to make shapes from a ground of paint. The shapes were then enhanced with mixed media, mostly oil based, layered in a dry brush fashion.

The type is Scala, an old style, neohumanist serif typeface created in 1990 by Dutch typeface designer Martin Majoor.